# AYRSHIRE TRACTION

## Colin J. Howat

AMBERLEY

First published 2015

Amberley Publishing
The Hill, Stroud
Gloucestershire, GL5 4EP

www.amberley-books.com

Copyright © Colin J. Howat, 2015

The right of Colin J. Howat to be identified as
the Author of this work has been asserted in
accordance with the Copyrights, Designs and
Patents Act 1988.

ISBN 978 1 4456 5083 8 (print)
ISBN 978 1 4456 5084 5 (ebook)

British Library Cataloguing in Publication Data.
A catalogue record for this book is available from
the British Library.

Typesetting by Amberley Publishing.
Printed in the UK.

# Introduction

For some people the end of steam in the 1960s meant the end of the railway, and in some respects this was true. Decisions made as far back as the early 1950s are still having an impact today. After Dr Beeching made his recommendations, the government of the day were faced with running down steam and replacing most services with diesel traction and in some cases electric. When I was growing up in the 1960s I had no real appreciation of this rundown, but by the time I was five years old I can vaguely remember some of the old steam locos chuffing their way past my home town of Irvine, heading back to Ayr depot. I was more interested in playing football with my friends. However, by 1965 I can remember travelling from Irvine to Glasgow St Enoch station, which closed the following year. I also remember when the Ayrshire services were switched to Glasgow Central in June 1966.

In the 1965–74 period I travelled from my home town of Irvine to Glasgow on many occasions to visit family relations. At this time, the vast bulk of Ayr–Glasgow services were in the hands of the Inter-City DMUs, later classified Class 126. It was a great adventure and I can just about remember arriving at the old Glasgow St Enoch station and travelling over the long-closed Kilbarchan Loop line between Elderslie, south of Paisley, and Brownhill, just north of Dalry. I think this is what fostered a basic interest in railways, and I always looked forward to these family excursions. At the time, British Rail had just suffered the ravages of Dr Beeching and many lines were about to disappear into oblivion. For example, in about 1966 I can remember standing at Dreghorn level crossing, near Irvine, with my father, watching a freight train operated by a BR Standard Mogul steam engine shunting mineral wagons into the local sidings, not realising that this was one of the last trains in the area. A few years later this line was lifted, the track bed was sold off and new motorways and various retail developments were built over the line, thus precluding any chance of the Irvine–Kilmarnock line ever being reopened. I also remember standing at an overbridge in Cunninghamhead, on the outskirts of Irvine, overlooking the Dalry–Kilmarnock line and observing a car transporter service in 1968. I later worked out that this was one of the Linwood–Luton Cartic trains, which were again taken for granted at the time. Like the mines, factories and various other heavy industries, this heritage in the west of Scotland would disappear forever. Such was the case in much of Ayrshire, and it was not until the 1980s that local councils and certain government officials began to realise that what railways were left were worth keeping, and so a spate of station reopenings began to take place.

In 1984, Kilmaurs and Auchinleck were both reopened; New Cumnock reopened in 1991 and Sanquhar in 1994. Sadly, in recent years, mainly due to a lack of funding, opportunities such as Mauchline and Cumnock have been postponed. On a more positive note, in Ayrshire itself a 5-mile section between Stewarton and Lugton on the main line between Kilmarnock and Glasgow Central was redoubled in 2009, but why it was not extended to Kilmarnock leaves me totally baffled. The main Ayr–Glasgow St Enoch and later Glasgow Central services were dominated by DMUs from 1959, with the Inter-City Diesel Multiple Units being the main force. Other Classes from 101 to 120 played a supporting role. The 126s worked between Ayrshire and Glasgow from 1959 until final withdrawal in 1983.

An attempt was made in the early 1960s to try and cut operating costs by the introduction of railbuses over various branch lines, but again most of these cross-country branch lines were closing anyway as the resident government of the day decided that they were not profitable enough to keep. Railbuses were trialled between Ayr and Dalmellington, Ardrossan, to Darvel via Kilmarnock and various other branch lines but were not successful as they were rough to ride and broke down quite frequently. By the late 1960s Class 126 DMUs were still the mainstay of passenger services, with Classes 101–116 also working between Kilmarnock and Glasgow Central and between Largs/Ardrossan Harbour and Glasgow Central. The main Glasgow and South Western (G&SW) route between Carlisle and Glasgow Central via Dumfries and Kilmarnock was worked by a mixture of Class 25–27 diesel locos, with occasional appearances of other classes such as Class 37 and 47 locos. Carlisle Kingmoor-based Derby Lightweight units also appeared from time to time, with occasional appearances by the heavier Derby Class 108 two-car units. From May 1970, Class 50s appeared on top link passenger duties between Glasgow Central and London Euston services as far as Crewe, where electric traction took over. These powerful diesels were also to be seen on Freightliner and various other duties.

The period between 1970 and 1974 was particularly busy in Ayrshire, as the West Coast Main Line between Motherwell and Carlisle via Carstairs was closed for engineering work for long periods in connection with electrification work, making the G&SW line even busier. The Class 40/45/46s were also in use, but from 1981 were banned by BR track engineers into Glasgow Central station due to the complex track layout known as the 'jungle', which had made the peaks very prone to derailments. In fact, after a third loco was derailed around 1981, the Class 40/45/46s were all barred from Glasgow Central. In 1983, after the Class 126 DMUs were withdrawn, Classes 101–120 took over until electrification came in from September 1986. With the gradual withdrawal of Class 126 units, Class 101, 107 and 116 units from Hamilton depot came in to replace them. The long distance Stranraer Harbour–Glasgow Central services went over to loco hauling, with a mixture of various diesel classes from 25–47 being supplied. However, in March 1986 a major setback occurred when all Class 107 units were stopped on account of axle problems. BR Scottish Region were faced with drafting in various other DMU classes from numerous depots in England to cover. This included Class 105s from Norwich, Class 120s from Derby and Cardiff and Class 108s from Leeds Nelville Hill depot. This produced weird and wonderful unit and livery combinations known locally as the 'Frankenstein' units. The axle problem was eventually solved around May 1986. In September 1986, electric units with Class 318s finally took over the main Glasgow to Ayr workings, although a DMU shuttle remained between Ardrossan South Beach and Largs. This existed until the overheads were switched on between Ardrossan, South Beach and Largs from January 1987. The 318s worked both Glasgow Central–Ayr/Largs and Ardrossan Harbour services. In 1996, Class 303 units were introduced on a limited Ayrshire working on a Glasgow Central–Ardrossan South Beach peak-hour evening service only. The 303s were only used if Class 318s failed or there had been extreme shortages. The 303s were also used during the Open golf at Troon in 1997 when golf specials ran between Glasgow Central and Troon. The Class 311s, which were also based at Shields depot in Glasgow, never ran in traffic in Ayrshire, but after they were converted for use as Sandite units they did run as reclassified 936 units. They were frequent visitors between 1990 and 1996. I remember the first winter when the 318s were in service, and in January 1987 there was heavy snowfall in Ayrshire and temperatures dropped to below -10 degrees Celsius. As a result, the new 318s struggled with door problems and drivers found it increasingly difficult to open them. Consequently, a number of Class 303s were drafted in to help out, but of course they did not have a toilet on board.

Class 314s that are also based at Shields depot, which were (and to this day are) mainly used in the south Glasgow area, visit Ayrshire very infrequently. However, in the winter of 2009/2010, again due to adverse weather conditions, they were used to Ayr and Largs, causing some local services in the Glasgow area to be cancelled. This was mainly due to the poor availability of Class 334 units.

Eventually, from May 2010 the Class 334s were diagrammed alongside the older Class 318s, until they themselves were transferred away to the Glasgow Northclyde area. They were then replaced by the newer Class 380s from May 2011.

On the east side of Ayrshire, on the diesel route between Carlisle and Glasgow Central, Class 47 loco-hauled trains were the mainstay until they were displaced by Class 156 diesel units that took over the Glasgow Central–Carlisle/Newcastle services from September 1988. Some local services remained in use with DMUs, but by 1993 all local and long distance services were in the hands of Class 156 units.

On the freight side, in the late 1970s Ayrshire had many diesel locos – from humble Class 08 shunters to main line Class 90s. The 08s were based at Ayr with three also out based at Ardrossan Harbour. Double-headed Class 20 locos were a common site all around Ayrshire working local trip trains. However, eventually, with the rundown of freight most of the early diesel classes would be eliminated as the industry concentrated on bulk movements, such as coal and containers, and the days of local pick up freights with a Class 20 or 25 and a brake van visiting a local factory or yard were well and truly over. By the mid-1990s, most of the coal traffic around Ayrshire was in the hands of Class 56 locos based at Motherwell, with six to seven locos out based at Ayr depot. These worked along with the older Class 26s and 37s but they themselves were gradually replaced by more powerful Class 60s from 1995. Further changes took place when English Welsh & Scottish Railways (EWS) decided to bring in Class 66 locos from America from the General Motor Company. These locos started to appear in Ayrshire from August 1998. In recent years, due to a number of opencast mine closures at Knockshinnoch and Waterside, EWS, the main freight operator now known as DB Schenker (DBS), have lost a lot of the freight flows. This has also been due in part to stiffer competition from Freightliner Heavy Haul and GB Railfreight and a slight downturn in the coal market. However, most coal trains are now running from Hunterston Clydeport to various power stations in England, and there is also an internal Scottish flow running from Hunterston to Longannet power station in Fife.

To conclude, I must admit that I was sad when DBS shut down Ayr depot in May 2010, and was even sadder to see the demolition squads working around the depot towards the end of 2014. However, hopefully this book will convey a taste of both the passenger and freight traction services around Ayrshire from 1974 to the present day.

A Park Royal railbus at Crosshouse station with an Ardrossan–Kilmarnock working. These services were covered by steam trains until 1959, when the railbuses were introduced. The tracks on the right went to Dalry and on to Paisley. This was the original main line from Kilmarnock to Glasgow St Enoch before the more direct route between Kilmarnock and Barrhead was opened in 1876. This line was finally closed in May 1976. The track on the left to Ardrossan is now a cycle pathway as far as Irvine. Taken around 1962. (Alec Clarke/C. Howat Collection)

A six-car Class 126 DMU near Bogside, north of Irvine, with the 14.10 Ayr–Glasgow Central train, my first official railway photograph, taken with a Kodac Instamatic camera. You can just about see the headcode '1A38' on the front of the train. These were phased out from 1976. Taken July 1974.

Maintenance supervisor Willie Carlyle at Ayr depot after fixing one of his beloved Class 126 power cars, No. SC 51040. Class 126 units could not provide through air or electrical feeds when tied up to other DMU classes or electrics due to their unique characteristics. They could, however, be pushed or hauled with the buckeye dropped to clear the main line. This contributed to their demise in 1983. Taken May 1978.

No. 25082 (Glasgow Eastfield) crosses the river Irvine with an advertised day-return excursion from Irvine to Dalmuir Park, near Clydebank, for a school outing. The children were at Irvine to visit the Magnum Leisure Centre. Taken June 1979.

A three-car Class 101 DMU at Bogside, north of Irvine, with the 11.15 Ayr–Glasgow Central service. The early Glasgow Passenger Transport Livery (PTE), which was white coaches and a blue strip, was brought in around 1977 but was eventually phased out in the early 1980s. Several Class 101 sets were allocated to Ayr on and off from the 1960s and played a supporting role to the main Class 126 sets. Taken July 1979.

A three-car Class 107 DMU at Barassie with the 1935 Glasgow Central–Ayr via Kilmarnock service. This was one of the few trains that ran this route at this time that allowed travel between Kilmarnock and Ayr. Taken July 1979.

A six-car Class 126 DMU at Barassie Junction with the 09.15 Ayr–Glasgow Central service. Note that the motor-brake coaches still had end gangways, which allowed passengers through access when coupled up. These started to be removed from October 1979 due to drivers complaining of draughts. The last coach to be done was No. SC 51027 in January 1981. Taken June 1979.

A six-car Class 126 DMU near Lochgreen, on the Troon-avoiding line, with the 10.42 Glasgow Central–Stranraer Harbour service. This was the only booked passenger service that used the line at this time. The Troon-avoiding lines were taken out of use in January 1983, when resignalling in connection with electrification of the Ayrshire area began. There is still part of the route available for freight trains to use, with approximately a mile of double track left. These tracks are still used by both Freightliner and GB Railfreight. Taken July 1979.

A six-car Class 101 at Lochgreen, south of Troon, with the 10.45 Ayr–Glasgow Central service. Royal Troon golf course is to the right. Lochgreen signal box closed when colour-light signalling came in from January 1983. Taken June 1979.

No. 47555 *The Commonwealth Spirit* (Crewe diesel depot) at Kilmarnock with the 14.30 Carlisle–Stranraer Harbour service, locally known at the time as the 'Midday Paddy'. This loco was named at London St Pancras on 9 April 1979. Taken July 1979.

A Class 25 on Stewarton viaduct with the 08.40 Carlisle–Glasgow Central via Dumfries and Kilmarnock service. This track was singled in 1974 as part of the west coast rationalisation. There was a proposal to close this line completely between Barrhead and Kilmarnock, with services running between Kilmarnock and Glasgow via Crosshouse and Dalry. However, around 1975 the residents of Stewarton objected, and, after several public meetings, BR were forced to retain the line, albeit as a single track with a crossing loop at Lugton. However, this went on to prove to be one of the costliest short term measures ever made, with constant late running due to limited capacity. Part of this line was re-doubled between Stewarton and Lugton in 2009, including this viaduct. However, the local service was also upgraded from hourly to half-hourly, causing the same operational problems. Taken July 1979.

A six-car Class 116 DMU at Glengarnock with the 10.15 Glasgow Central–Largs service. Note the abutments in the background for the former Caledonian liner, which crossed over the main line to another station at Kilbirnie. This was the line from Glasgow to Kilbirnie, via Neilston and Giffen. This was closed to passengers in the early 1930s. The Class 116 units were based at Hamilton depot and worked mainly from Glasgow to Kilmacolm, Shotts, Edinburgh, Largs and Ardrossan and very rarely strayed onto Ayr services. Taken July 1979.

No. 20020 (Glasgow Eastfield) on the Giffen branch, near Beith, with the weekly naval armament train from Giffen to Mossend Yard, near Glasgow. This line was closed in 1987 but most of the track is still in place, albeit very overgrown. The connection to the main Kilmarnock to Barrhead line at Lugton line was severed in December 2009 when the re-doubling between Lugton and Stewarton was done. Taken July 1979.

No. 56065 (Sheffield Tinsley) approaching Lochside with a test train of iron ore wagons from Ravenscraig to Hunterston. At this time the Ravenscraig services were in the hands of pairs of Class 37s. The Class 56 was brought up for a trial run, but apparently it was not successful as it struggled up the steep gradient at Bellshill on the south side of Glasgow. The Class 56s were never used again on these workings. However, in the mid-1990s they were used on the Hunterston to Longannet workings that avoided the Bellshill bank. Taken December 1979.

A nine-car Class 126 DMU pulls away from Irvine with the 06.32 Girvan–Glasgow Central service. At this time, all services were booked to be either 3-, 6- or 9-car sets, although occasional variations to this occurred. Taken October 1979.

No. 45057 (Nottingham Toton) at Kilmarnock with the 10.30 Nottingham–Glasgow Central service – a remnant of the old Thames Clyde express, which used to run all the way from London St Pancras to Glasgow St Enoch. Taken August 1979.

A nine-car Class 126 DMU at Bogside with the 10.42 Glasgow Central–Stranraer Harbour service. Note that by this time the route indicator boxes were not getting used. The indicator boxes were displayed with the train headcode to assist each signal box as to the destination of each train. However, by the mid-1970s modern signalling centres were beginning to render them irrelevant. They are still in use today and are the main form of train identification in modern signalling centres. Taken July 1977.

A two-car Class 126 DMU at Irvine with the 14.35 Glasgow Central–Ayr service. Normally the Class 126s worked in 3-, 6- or 9-car mode, but, due to a defective trailer (middle coach), on this occasion only 2 power cars were in use. Taken March 1981.

A six-car Class 126 DMU in the snow at Irvine with the 13.15 Ayr–Glasgow Central service. Note the old railway workshops in the background in Irvine Yard, now all gone and replaced by a retail park. Taken February 1980.

A six-car Class 126 DMU on the Troon-avoiding line, at the site of the original Troon station, with the 11.35 Glasgow Central–Stranraer service. The original station was brought into use when the Ayr to Glasgow St Enoch line opened in 1841. However, because it was situated approximately 2 miles away from the main part of the town, it was closed to passengers in 1905, although it remained in use for goods traffic until 1963. Taken March 1980.

No. 156477 (Glasgow Corkerhill) north of New Cumnock with the 13.10 Carlisle–Glasgow Central service. Note the unit in First Group livery. Taken May 2005.

A five-car Class 221 Voyager sits mid-road at Kilmarnock with a diverted Birmingham New Street–Glasgow Central service. This train had been diverted via Dumfries and Kilmarnock due to engineering operations on the West Coast Main Line north of Carlisle. Taken February 2004.

Virgin Class 57 also at Kilmarnock, coupled up to DVT/Virgin MK3 coaches with a dead Class 87 on rear, on a diverted London Euston–Glasgow Central service. The driver had been speaking to the signaller and was awaiting a Class 156 to clear the single line from Lugton. This has been the bane of this line since 1974. Taken February 2004.

A six-car 314 EMU at Kilwinning in the snow, working the 12.52 Largs to Glasgow Central service. Train formed by Nos 314212 and 314214 (both Glasgow Shields).

These units do not normally work in Ayrshire, but because of poor class 318 availability, they were rushed into service to help out. Taken December 1999.

No. 09103 (Motherwell) at Ayr harbour shunting MGR wagons. Most shunting in and around Falkland Yard were in the hands of Class 08 locos until the mid-1990s. From 1996 a mixture of Class 08 and 09 shunters worked together until Class 09s were the sole shunters until DBS closed Ayr depot in 2010. Taken April 2005.

A six-car Class 334 EMU south of Glengarnock with the 10.30 Glasgow Central–Ayr service. The Class 334s had many teething problems in the early days and originally were to be introduced in 2000. However, they did not enter squadron service until late 2001. They were originally intended as replacements for the Class 318s, but in fact worked alongside them between Glasgow Central and Ayrshire until they were also replaced by the newer Class 380s from 2011. Taken March 2004.

No. 156403, borrowed from Central Trains due to a Scotrail Class 156 unit shortage at Kilmarnock, having just arrived on a service from Girvan. This unit was on hire to Scotrail for approximately three months. Taken June 2006.

No. 40145, privately owned, at Kilmarnock station with an SRPS excursion from Carlisle to Oban. Class 40s were common in Ayrshire and worked both passenger and freight trains. However, they were gradually replaced by more powerful Class 47s on all services from 1984 onwards. Taken August 2007.

No. 60068 (Toton Nottingham) at Kilwinning with the 14.33 Prestwick Airport–Grangemouth Terminal empty aviation tank train. Most of the Class 60 fleet was withdrawn the following year, although some are making a comeback with COLAS and DBS. Taken December 2008.

No. 66509 (Leeds Freightliner) at Annbank Junction with a Killoch–Drax loaded coal train. The line to the left is the direct freight line between Mauchline Junction and Ayr. Both these lines are still busy today. Taken April 2009.

A six-car Class 334 EMU at Gailes, south of Irvine, with the 15.00 Glasgow Central–Ayr service. Western Gailes golf course is on the left; Glasgow Gailes golf course to the right. Taken September 2009.

No. 67027 (Nottingham Toton) at Irvine with the empty slurry tanks from the Irvine Caledonian pulp mill, near Barassie to Mossend working. These tanks are then sent via the West Coast Main Line to the Channel Tunnel and on to Antwerp docks in Belgium. Taken September 2009.

No. 156456 (Glasgow Corkerhill) arrives at a cold Kilmarnock with the 09.03 service from Glasgow Central to Carlisle. It was at least -15 degrees Celsius, and so cold that the destination screen on the unit could hardly be seen. Taken January 2010.

No. 156434 (Glasgow Corkerhill), still in maroon PTE livery, on the recently re-doubled track between Lugton and Stewarton with the 08.42 Glasgow Central–Kilmarnock service. The maroon livery was introduced from the late 1990s and replaced the original Strathclyde orange livery. Taken January 2010.

No. 156430 (Glasgow Corkerhill) near Kilmaurs, on the single line between Stewarton and Kilmarnock, with the 11.12 Glasgow Central–Kilmarnock service. This unit had recently been repainted with the latest Scotrail saltire livery. Taken March 2010.

Nos 37607 and 37421 (Both DRS Carlisle) at Irvine with a Pathfinders Easter railtour from London Euston to Stranraer. Taken April 2010.

No. 66131 (Nottingham Toton) approaches Hillhouse, near Barassie, with an empty MGR from Ratcliffe power station, bound for Falkland Yard. Taken April 2010.

A six-car Class 334 EMU, unit 039 leading, at Gailes, between Irvine and Barassie, with the 10.00 Glasgow Central–Ayr service. Taken April 2010.

A six-car Class 334 EMU, unit 027 leading, at Kilwinning with the 09.30 Glasgow Central–Ayr service. Passenger numbers steadily increased from the 1990s, so much so that the half-hourly services became mainly six-cars-vice-three from 2006. By December 2012, a revised fifteen-minute service frequency had been introduced to meet passenger demand. Taken May 2010.

No. 66104 (Nottingham Toton) at Riccarton, near Kilmarnock, with empty oil tanks heading back to Grangemouth oil terminal. At one time this track continued south of Kilmarnock, making it possible to travel to Ayr via Kilmarnock without having to reverse in Kilmarnock station. However, once again due to the Beeching cuts in the 1960s, this track was lifted beyond Riccarton. Taken May 2010.

No. 47739 (COLAS) *Robin of Templecombe* at Kilmarnock Barclay Works. This loco had arrived earlier in the week with MK3 Great Western coaches for refurbishment. These coaches had been brought all the way from Laira, in Plymouth. Taken June 2010.

No. 70003 (Leeds Freightliner) near Troon with empty MGR working from Eggborough power station to Killoch Colliery. The Class 70s are not common in Ayrshire but were regularly seen between 2009 and 2012 at various locations. Taken July 2010.

A four-car Class 156 crosses Stewarton viaduct with the 09.12 Glasgow Central–Carlisle service. Class 156s go virtually anywhere in central Scotland, and at one time worked between Inverness and the far north and Kyle lines, until replaced by Class 158s. Taken June 2010.

No. 156436 (Glasgow Corkerhill) crosses over the reconstructed bridge south of Stewarton with the 09.42 Glasgow Central–Kilmarnock service. The original bridge had been destroyed by a Grangemouth to Riccarton aviation fuel train the previous year. The structure had given way as the train passed over it. Fortunately there were no fatalities. However, Kilmarnock–Glasgow Central services were severely disrupted for approximately three months, resulting in all Carlisle–Glasgow Central services having to be diverted via Barassie and Paisley. Taken June 2010.

No. 66108 (Nottingham Toton) near Troon with the afternoon Prestwick to Grangemouth empty aviation fuel train. The old Troon Harbour branch veered off to the right, but now it has now been built on and is very difficult to see. Barassie Works, which closed in 1973, was off camera to the left. Taken July 2010.

Two Direct Rail services (DRS) Class 66s with the nuclear flask train at Brownhill, between Dalry and Glengarnock, en route from Hunterston to Sellafield reprocessing plant in Cumbria. Taken September 2010.

Sandite Machine DR 98955, owned by Network Rail, at Brownhill, north of Dalry, en route to Mossend from Falkland Yard. These machines are normally only seen from November to March when sanding the tracks to assist all stopping and departing trains at stations as required. This machine was out running for driver training. Taken September 2010.

No. 66707 (Doncaster GBRF) *Sir Sam Fay Great Central Railway* at Brownhill Loop with an empty MGR from Drax to Hunterston. This train was being looped for passage of electrics. Taken September 2010.

No. 66201 (Nottingham Toton) at Brownhill, heading north with a loaded MGR from Hunterston to Longannet power station. Taken September 2010.

No. 66724 (Doncaster GBRF) at Drax power station near Stevenston, with a Hunterston–Drax loaded MGR. Note the Isle of Arran in the background. Taken September 2010.

Five-car Voyager near Kilmaurs with a diverted Glasgow Central–Birmingham New Street service. Note the distant colour light signal belonging to Lugton signal box behind the rear coach, applicable to northbound trains. This line was singled in 1974. Taken November 2010.

No. 221101 (Central Rivers Burton Upon Trent) *Louis Bleriot* at Stewarton, heading north with a diverted Birmingham New Street–Glasgow Central service. The Voyager had been diverted due to engineering works on the West Coast Main Line near Carstairs. Taken November 2010.

EMU No. 334006 (Glasgow Shields) in the snow at Dalry with the 14.15 Glasgow Central–Ardrossan Harbour service. This was a particularly bad winter and many Class 334s struggled with the conditions. Taken December 2010.

EMU No. 318270 (Glasgow Shields) also in the snow at Dalry with the 13.52 Largs–Glasgow Central service. The end gangways were removed and welded up in the mid-2000s when the units were refurbished at Barclays of Kilmarnock. Taken December 2010.

No. 66104 (Nottingham Toton) at Gailes, near Irvine, with the Prestwick Airport–Grangemouth aviation fuel empties. This service generally runs once a week. Taken January 2011.

No. 70002 (Leeds Freightliner) at Ballochmyle, between Auchinleck and Mauchline, with a Ratcliffe power station–Killoch empty MGR. Freightliner tried out the Class 70s for a few years but they have rarely been seen in Scotland since 2012. Taken January 2011.

No. 66164 (Nottingham Toton) near Gatehead, between Kilmarnock and Barassie, with empty MGR from Falkland Yard to Knockshinnoch. The first railway line in Scotland is adjacent to this line (behind the camera position) and the original viaduct is still in site as a heritage attraction. Taken March 2011.

EMU No. 380008 (Glasgow Shields) approaches Saltcoats with the 14.15 Glasgow Central–Ardrossan Harbour service. This is the section of line that is closed frequently due to high waves splashing onto the overheads, causing them to trip out. Taken May 2011.

No. 70006 (Leeds Freightliner) at Falkland Yard, en route from Drax power station to Hunterston. Note the graffiti on the brick signalling building, which is becoming increasingly common throughout the whole rail network. Taken May 2011.

EMU No. 380018 (Glasgow Shields) passes Kilbirnie Loch, north of Glengarnock, with an Ardrossan Town–Glasgow Central service. There was an additional double-tracked line around the opposite side of the loch known as the Kilbarchan Loop line. This ran a parallel course from Elderslie to Brownhill but was closed in 1972 and most of it is now a cycle path. Taken July 2011.

Virgin Class 57 at Barony, north of Auchinleck, with a drivers' trainer. The loco was running from Carlisle to Polmadie depot in Glasgow and presumably training Polmadie-based Virgin drivers. Taken July 2011.

No. 66097 (Nottingham Toton) in the new DBS livery at Polquhap summit, north of New Cumnock, with a loaded MGR working from Greenbank to West Burton power station. The train heads north to sidings north of Kilmarnock station, known as the 'Long Lyes', where the Class 66 runs round its train and then heads back south. Taken September 2011.

No. 37066 (Thornaby) at Kilmarnock with a Carlisle Kingmoor–Mossend freight. This freight was booked to cross a southbound freight, which would be signalled into platform No. 4. Nowadays it is virtually impossible for freight trains and diverted Virgin services to get a path due to the constraints of the single line between Kilmarnock and Stewarton (Lockridge Junction). Taken March 1982.

EMU No. 380113 (Glasgow Shields) approaching Dalry with the 11.45 Glasgow Central–Largs service. This section of track used to be four tracks all the way from Brownhill, south of Glengarnock, to Kilwinning. It was cut back to Dalry in the 1960s and further cut back to just north of Dalry station when the Ayrshire electrification was brought in from September 1986. Taken November 2011.

No. 67030 (Nottingham Toton) at Auchinleck with a northbound drivers' trainer for Polmadie-based Virgin drivers. The loco was en route from Carlisle to Polmadie. Note the saltire sticker on front of loco above the loco number. Taken June 2012.

EMU No. 380011 (Glasgow Shields) at Stevenston level crossing with the 13.36 Ardrossan Harbour–Glasgow Central service. Stevenston had two stations at one time, the second being on the former Caledonian route from Kilwinning to Ardrossan Montgomerie Pier. The second station was known as Stevenston Moor Park and was closed in 1956. Taken September 2012.

A two-car Class 156 crosses the river Irvine on Campbells bridge, north of Irvine, with the 14.37 Stranraer–Glasgow Central service. Taken November 2012.

A six-car Class 380 EMU approaches Irvine with the 08.30 Glasgow Central–Ayr service. Note how close the overhead stanchions are located, due to the strong winds experienced frequently in this area. Taken April 2013.

A four-car Class 380 EMU south of West Kilbride with the 11.52 Largs–Glasgow Central service. The Largs line still only has an hourly service to Glasgow Central mainly due to the single line constraints after Ardrossan South Beach. Taken April 2013.

EMU No. 380006 (Glasgow Shields) south of Largs at 'The Pen', which refers to the Viking ruin in the background, with the 12.52 Largs–Glasgow Central service. Taken April 2013.

No. 66507 (Leeds Freightliner) near New Cumnock with the 0936 Hunterston–Drax power station loaded coal service. Hunterston port on the west coast of Scotland is still playing an important part in rail operations, with many ships from as far afield as South Africa and Australia bringing in imported coal. Taken April 2013.

No. 156509 (Glasgow Corkerhill) near New Cumnock with the 11.10 Carlisle–Glasgow Central service. Greenbank opencast mine and the now-closed Knockshinnoch site are both located to the right just beyond the small fishing loch. Taken April 2013.

Deltic Class No. 55022 near Gatehead, west of Kilmarnock, with a Kilmarnock Brodie Works–Yoker via Barassie working with a recently refurbished Class 334 EMU in new Scotrail saltire livery. Taken May 2013.

No. 66548 (Leeds Freightliner) at Pennyburn on the single line between Dubbs Junction and Byrehill Junction, south of Kilwinning, with the 10.10 Hunterston–Drax loaded MGR. This spur only sees freight trains and Scotrail empty coaching stock moves. It was used by through Ardrossan–Kilmarnock railbuses until passenger services were withdrawn in 1964. Taken July 2013.

No. 66750 (COLAS) at Kilmarnock with a COLAS driver trainer. COLAS took over the Riccarton–Grangemouth oil tank workings from DBS in September 2013. Taken July 2013.

No. 56105 (COLAS) crosses the River Irvine north of Irvine with the weekly Prestwick Airport–Grangemouth Yard empty aviation tank service. Taken September 2013.

EMU No. 380113 (Glasgow Shields) near West Kilbride, heading north with the 09.45 Glasgow Central–Largs service. Only one track is electrified between Ardrossan South Beach and Hunterston. Note Firth of Clyde in background, with Ailsa Craig island also visible. Taken October 2013.

A close up of EMUs Nos 380003/013 (both Glasgow Shields depot) coupled up. The coupling up of 380 sets takes at least five minutes due to various interlocking doors. Taken June 2014.

The 'Yellow Banana', otherwise known as the Network Rail Measurement Train. This train visits most areas in the UK and is seen here in the mid-road at Kilmarnock awaiting a path to Lugton en route from Derby to Craigentinny, near Edinburgh. Taken June 2014.

No. 66419 (Leeds Freightliner), still in original DRS livery, near New Cumnock with a northbound empty MGR from Carlisle Kingmoor Yard to Killoch Colliery. Taken June 2014.

Deltic No. 55022 at Gailes near Irvine with a Yoker–Kilmarnock Brodie Works via Barassie move with another Class 334 for refurbishment. Taken August 2014.

Deltic No. 55022 takes the single line to Kilmarnock at Barassie Junction with the regular Yoker–Kilmarnock Brodie Works working with a Class 334 for refurbishment. This contract finished in September 2014. Taken August 2014.

Deltic No. 55022 couples up to tanks at Kilmarnock after running round its train that had departed from Kilmarnock Brodie Works. The tanks are coupled with the refurbished Class 334 to assist brake force. The train then runs to Yoker via Barassie and the Class 334 will eventually be returned to Scotrail at Glasgow Shields depot. Taken August 2014.

EMU No. 380107 (Glasgow Shields) at Gailes with the 16.05 Ayr–Glasgow Central service. The train is doing approximately 90 mph. Taken November 2012.

No. 66746 (Doncaster GBRF) at Pennyburn, south of Kilwinning, with an empty MGR Tyne Yard–Hunterston service. GB Railfreight are now beginning to take more coal traffic away from DBS. Taken February 2015.

Withdrawn from service, EMU No. 311101, which had worked mainly in the Glasgow electric network from 1967 until 1990, lying in Falkland Yard, Ayr, en route to being scrapped. There was talk in the mid-1980s of 311s being upgraded with toilets, for use on the new Ayrshire electrified services but this did not happen. Taken November 1990.

No. 66159 (Nottingham Toton) near New Cumnock with a northbound Knockshinnoch–Drax MGR service. This working goes north to Kilmarnock sidings, reverses and then heads back south. Taken May 2005.

No. 66196 (Nottingham Toton) on Ballochmyle viaduct, south of Mauchline, with a northbound MGR. At one time, this viaduct had the highest span of any railway bridge in the UK at well over 150 feet. Taken May 2005.

No. 66171 (Nottingham Toton) on the Greenburn branch near New Cumnock with a loaded MGR for Ratcliffe power station. Greenburn opencast mine opened in 2003 and has taken over all coal traffic from the closed Knockshinnoch mine, which was located approximately a mile away, since 2010. Taken May 2005.

No. 66050 (Nottingham Toton) on the Knockshinnoch branch with empty MGR nearing its destination. Knockshinnoch closed in 2010. Taken May 2005.

An unidentified Class 66 in the Nith valley, north of Mauchline near Mossgiel Tunnel, with a mixed freight Falkland Yard–Carlisle Kingmoor Yard service heading south. Robert Burns, the famous Scottish poet, rented Mossgiel farm near this location. Taken June 2004.

No. 66092 (Nottingham Toton), near Mossblown, on the single line from Annbank Junction to Mauchline with an empty MGR Falkland Yard–Knockshinnoch service. Taken June 2005.

No. 09103 (Motherwell) at Falkland Yard shunting empty MGRs on the west side of the yard. This loco started life numbered as D3934 and moved from Thornaby to Motherwell in November 1993. Taken May 2006.

EMU No. 334001 (Glasgow Shields) was given the name of the late First Minister of Scotland, *Donald Dewar*. This is a close up of the nameplate on the side of unit. Taken March 2004.

No. 60020 (Nottingham Toton) at Falkland Yard with aviation tanks for Prestwick Airport. This train had arrived from Grangemouth and the Class 60 ran around in Falkland Yard before heading back north to Prestwick. Taken March 2004.

No. 66205 (Nottingham Toton) surrounded by autumn leaves at Kay Park Junction, south of Kilmarnock, with a loaded MGR from Knockshinnoch to Drax power station. Taken November 2004.

No. 66059 (Nottingham Toton) approaches Newton-on-Ayr Junction with an empty MGR Ayr Harbour–Chalmerston train. Chalmerston opencast mine closed in 2010. The line is still in situ but its future looks doubtful. Taken April 2004.

A six-car Class 334 EMU approaches Kilwinning, unit 026 leading, with the 13.00 Glasgow Central–Ayr service. At this time, all Ayrshire services were worked by a mixture of Class 318 and 334 units. Taken April 2002.

A six-car Class 318 EMU, unit 263 leading, at Kilwinning with the 14.00 Glasgow Central–Ayr service. Taken April 2002.

No. 66047 (Nottingham Toton) near West Kilbride with the 19.46 Hunterston–Longannet loaded MGR service. This was just after the larger HTA 100-ton wagons had been introduced, replacing the conventional 45 ton wagons. Taken April 2002.

A six-car Class 334 EMU, unit 031 leading, at Irvine with the 09.30 Glasgow Central–Ayr service. Taken May 2002.

A six-car Class 126 DMU at Bogside, north of Irvine, with the 13.45 Ayr–Glasgow Central service. The leading power car was No. SC 79168, a former Edinburgh–Queen Street DMU transferred to Ayr in 1972. Several of these vehicles were moved to Ayr but most had gone by 1980. Taken October 1975.

A five-car Class 126 DMU at Bogside with the 11.00 Glasgow Central–Ayr service. One power car is missing, probably due to a failure. Bogside station was situated next to the nearby horse racing course. The Scottish Grand National was held here before it moved to Ayr in 1965. Bogside station itself closed in 1967. Taken November 1980.

A three-car Class 126 DMU, power car SC 51033 leading, arriving at Irvine with the 13.35 Glasgow Central–Ayr service. Taken October 1980.

No. 47570 (Crewe diesel depot) at St Quivox, east of Ayr, on the Mauchline–Ayr freight line with the Hertfordshire railtour, the Wigtonshire Wanderer, heading for Ardrossan Harbour. This section of line was singled in 1984. Taken November 1980.

A three-car Class 116 DMU at West Kilbride with the 11.52 Largs–Glasgow Central service. This station now only has one platform, although the remaining non-electrified track is still used by freight trains to and from Hunterston. Taken November 1980.

No. 47541 (Crewe diesel depot) at Prestwick Town with the 22.15 London Euston–Glasgow Central overnight sleeper service. This service was diverted away from Kilmarnock due to engineering works. It ran from Mauchline to Newton-on-Ayr, then northwards to Glasgow Central via Paisley Gilmour Street. Taken August 1981.

A three-car Class 107 DMU at Hunterston Low Level with a Branch Line Society railtour of Ayrshire. This railtour started from Glasgow Central and visited many branch lines around the county, also venturing into Renfrewshire. It eventually finished back at Glasgow Central. Taken August 1981.

A six-car Class 126 DMU at Maybole, power car SC 51034 trailing, with the 08.35 Glasgow Central–Stranraer Harbour service. Note the mail bags being exchanged from the guard's van area in the rear coach. Again a thing of the past. Taken August 1981.

No. 140001, the Leyland Experimental Vehicle, or LEV. This was the forerunner of the modern day pacers and sprinters. I had the misfortune of travelling on it on several occasions that summer and remember how bumpy it was at junctions. Taken August 1981.

Nos 20116 and 20146 (both Glasgow Eastfield) approach Irvine with an empty MGR from Longannet to Falkland Yard. At this time Barony Colliery, near Auchinleck, supplied the coal for Longannet. Barony mine closed in 1985. Taken August 1981.

No. 40012 (Manchester Longsight) at Kilmarnock with the 07.15 Nottingham–Glasgow Central service. The steam coming out the coaches indicates steam heating from the Class 40's boiler was working. Taken December 1981.

No. 46015 (Gateshead Newcastle) at Kilmarnock with the 12.40 Glasgow Central–Carlisle service. The Class 46 had worked up north from Carlisle on a diverted Manchester Piccadilly–Glasgow Central service, but, because Class 46s were not allowed into Glasgow Central, it was detached and replaced by a Class 47. The Class 46 was then reattached to the local service and headed back south to Carlisle. Taken March 1982.

A two-car Class 108 at Kilmarnock on the 06.10 Carlisle–Glasgow Central service. This service was normally booked to be a Class 47 with six MK1 coaches but the Class 47 had apparently failed at Carlisle, so the only traction available was a spare two-car Class 108 based at Carlisle Kingmoor. It was a tight squeeze all the way to Glasgow for commuters that day. Taken March 1982.

Nos 20191 and 25227 (both Glasgow Eastfield) at Kilmarnock with a Tyne Yard–Stranraer Harbour car train. All cars were exported to Northern Ireland. Taken February 1982.

No. 26037 (Inverness) at Kilmarnock with a local trip to Falkland Yard. The third wagon was a van containing whisky from the nearby Johnny Walker factory. These local trip workings are again a thing of the past. Taken February 1982.

A three-car Class 116 DMU at Kilwinning with an Ardrossan Harbour–Glasgow Central service. The Class 116 was based at Hamilton depot on the south side of Glasgow and these units primarily worked Glasgow Central–Ardrossan Harbour and Largs services. They only visited Ayr occasionally at this time. Taken April 1982.

No. 40057 (Gateshead Newcastle) at Dubbs Junction, south of Kilwinning. The Class 40 got the signal ahead of a six-car Class 107. The Class 40 was on an advertised day excursion from Manchester Victoria to Largs, and the six-car Class 107 was working the 12.15 Glasgow Central–Largs service. Taken April 1982.

No. 40057 (Gateshead Newcastle) at Largs with a return excursion to Manchester Victoria, plus an assortment of various DMUs. This station area has been completely transformed and only has two platforms left in use. Excursion trains are virtually a thing of the past. It is extremely difficult for additional trains to access Largs today due to the single line limitation from Ardrossan South Beach. Taken April 1982.

A three-car Class 126 DMU at Gatehead level crossing with the 14.00 Carlisle–Ayr service. Class 126 units were fairly uncommon on the main line south of Kilmarnock to Carlisle until September 1979, when a diagram was introduced leaving Ayr at 09.10. This lasted until the early 1980s, but reverted to loco hauling towards the end. Taken May 1982.

A three-car Class 101 DMU
at Brownhill, north of Dalry,
with a Largs–Glasgow Central
service. The sidings to the left
were just recently relaid to
provide a freight connection
to the nearby Roche chemical
works. Taken March 1982.

No. 47564 (Edinburgh
Haymarket) at Brownhill with
the weekly Grangemouth–
Riccarton oil tank service. This
section of track is now reduced
to two tracks, just about where
the train is located. Taken
April 1982.

A nine-car Class 126 DMU
takes the Troon-avoiding
line at Barassie Junction
with the 1135 Glasgow
Central–Stranraer Harbour
service. This line was closed
in January 1983, although
part of it has been retained
for freight traffic shunting.
Taken April 1982.

A three-car Class 101
DMU at Brownhill, north
of Dalry, with the 10.15
Ayr–Glasgow Central
service. The fields in the
background are now mainly
houses. Taken March 1982.

A six-car Class 126 DMU at Brownhill, near Glengarnock, with the 09.00 Glasgow Central–Girvan service. In the distance is Glengarnock steelworks, which was closed in 1985. Taken April 1982.

A six-car Class 107 DMU at Brownhill, south of Glengarnock, with the 08.26 Glasgow Central–Ardrossan Harbour service. Taken April 1982.

A three-car Class 126 DMU west of Kilmarnock, near Gatehead, with the 10.00 Stranraer Harbour–Kilmarnock service. Taken April 1982.

A nine-car Class 126 DMU at Brownhill, north of Dalry, with the 08.35 Glasgow Central–Stranraer Harbour service. Note how the second coach is tilting to the left. This was a characteristic of the trailer coaches because the seating was located on one side of the coach with the passageway down the opposite side. Taken April 1982.

No. 40081 (Healey Mills Wakefield) at Ardrossan Town with a return excursion from Ardrossan Harbour to Sunderland. Taken May 1982.

Nos 37292 and 37190 (Both Glasgow Eastfield) at Stevenston with empty iron ore hoppers from Ravenscraig to Hunterston. At this time iron ore, along with coal, was the staple diet of the Ravenscraig steelworks. However, the works closed amid much controversy in 1992. Taken May 1982.

No. 47462 (Glasgow Eastfield) at Lochgreen Junction with the 08.35 Glasgow Central–Stranraer Harbour service. The train is coming off the Troon-avoiding line. This was the first day of loco hauling replacing the Inter-City DMUs. Taken May 1982.

A six-car Class 107 DMU at Brownhill with the 19.52 Largs–Glasgow Central service. The Class 107s started life at Hamilton depot and were based there from 1961 until the depot closed in 1982. They were then transferred to Ayr. After electrification of the Ayr lines in 1986, they were sent to Glasgow Eastfield and Edinburgh Haymarket. However, most were withdrawn by the mid-1990s, except a few that lingered on as Sandite units; some are still in use on heritage lines. Taken June 1982.

No. 25057 (Manchester Longsight) at Dalry No. 2 signal box with empty coaching stock from Ardrossan Town to Corkerhill station, in connection with the papal visit. The Pope was at Bellahouston Park in Glasgow and there were special trains from all over Scotland converging on Corkerhill that day. Taken June 1982.

No. 37009 (Thornaby Tees) near Largs with a day excursion from Macclesfield to Largs. This line is now electrified but singled. Taken May 1982.

A six-car Class 126 DMU at Annbank Junction with the Swindon Diesel Preservation Society's railtour, which visited many branch lines. Here, the train is about to head east towards Mauchline. Class 126s very rarely ventured east towards Annbank except on the odd test run, so when the railtour came it was quite unusual. The signal box closed in August 1985 and the Annbank–Mauchline line was mothballed for two years. It was reopened in November 1987, albeit with a ground frame connection to the Killoch branch. Taken October 1982.

A three-car Class 105 DMU at Largs having just arrived on the 13.15 ex Glasgow Central. The yellow band above the front two windows indicates that the seating was still First Class. These units were drafted in, mainly from the Norwich area, to help out due a general DMU shortage at Ayr. They were only used for a few years until being dumped at Falkland Yard, Ayr, from 1987. Taken November 1982.

A three-car Class 107 DMU at Newton-on-Ayr with 08.10 SX (Saturdays excepted) Ayr–Glasgow Central service. Note the signal box on the overbridge. This box controlled movements to and from Ayr depot as well as the Annbank and Ayr Harbour branches. Taken August 1981.

No. 25221 (Manchester Longsight) at Fairlie High getting nuclear flasks loaded onto its wagons. The crane was operated by a Scottish Power representative and assisted by a BR railman who was brought out once a week, usually on a Wednesday. The flasks now arrive and depart from Hunterston Low Level and the service is operated by Carlisle based DRS. Taken May 1983.

No. 26040 (Inverness) at Mauchline with the 08.15 Carlisle–Glasgow Central service. The line coming in from the right is from Annbank Junction. Taken April 1983.

No. 40084 (Gateshead Newcastle) and No. 40068 (Healey Mills Wakefield) with possibly the longest passenger train in the modern era. This was a weekend railtour organised by Hertfordshire Railtours called the 'Skirl of the Pipes', which ran from Plymouth to various destinations in south-west Scotland, eventually finishing back in Bristol after a marathon four days. The two Class 40s were hauling seventeen MK1 coaches. Taken May 1983.

A two-car Class 108 DMU based at Carlisle Kingmoor, near Cumnock, with a special running from Carlisle to Kirkconnel due to engineering work in the Mauchline area. These units very rarely strayed north of Dumfries. Taken May 1983.

No. 27054 (Glasgow Eastfield) approaches Irvine with the 11.35 Glasgow Central–Stranrear Harbour service. Taken May 1983.

No. 20118 (Glasgow Eastfield) and No. 20139 (Edinburgh Haymarket) at Waterside on the Chalmerston branch, having just been loaded up with coal from the adjacent opencast site. The coal was then taken to Ayr harbour for onward shipment to Kilroot power station in Northern Ireland. Taken May 1983.

A six-car Class 107 DMU stabled in Ardrossan Town station. This station was closed in 1968 and used as a stabling point for DMUs until the station was reopened for passengers as part of the Ayrshire electrification project in September 1986. Taken May 1983.

Nos 37137 and 37155 (Both Motherwell) north of Ardrossan, heading an empty iron ore hopper train from Ravenscraig to Hunterston. Taken May 1983.

A six-car Class 116/101 DMU combination near West Kilbride with the 10.52 Largs–Glasgow Central service. Taken August 1983.

No. 08446 (Ayr depot) in Ardrossan Coal Yard with various coal bags. A friendly driver gave me a shot of driving the Class 08 in the yard. Now sadly all gone and closed. Taken June 1982.

EMU No. 314211 (Hyndland Glasgow) at Ayr depot in connection with the open day celebrations. Other unusual visitors included Deltic No. 55002, Steam loco No. 4471 *Flying Scotsman* and Class 87006 *City of Glasgow*. Taken October 1983.

MK1 coach SC 24848 painted in Sealink livery. This was an attempt by BR to attract more patronage on the Stranraer Harbour–Glasgow Central services. Here we see it stabled in Kyle Street, adjacent to Ayr station. The coaches were eventually replaced by more modern MK2 coaches from 1987. Kyle Street sidings were closed in 1986. Taken October 1983.

Deltic No. 55002, *The Kings Own Yorkshire Light Infantry,* owned by the National Railway Museum of York, on hand at Ayr depot. The loco was brought up dead inside the overnight Tyne–Stranraer Yard freight service for part of the open day celebrations at Ayr depot. Taken October 1983.

A three-car Class 104 DMU, power car M 53453 was brought up from Newton Heath, Manchester in January 1984 after a fire destroyed a number of Class 101 and 107 vehicles. This was it getting reformed into a new set prior to working in service at Ayr depot. Power car M 53453, plus another eight Class 104 vehicles, were brought up to help out. Taken January 1984.

No. 20110 and No. 20125 (both Eastfield) marshalled between two independent snow ploughs at Ayr depot. The locos had just returned from clearing snow drifts on the Chalmerston branch. Taken January 1984.

DMUs stabled in Kyle Street. This was handy for the station. However, when electrification came in, the sidings were closed in favour of new sidings at Townhead, south of the station. This area was converted into residential flats in 1989. Taken January 1984.

DMU Class 104 power car M 53505, still with its First Class compartment at the front of the unit, was another Class 104 drafted in by BR Scottish Region from Newton Heath, Manchester to cover for the fire damaged 101 and 107 units. Taken January 1984.

DMU Class 107 power car No. SC 52019 was one of seven coaches destroyed beyond repair, as can be seen, and was cannibalised for spare parts before heading for the scrapyard. The fire was started on Boxing Day 1983 and the civil police suspected that it was arson, although nobody was arrested. Taken January 1984.

No. 20114 (Glasgow Eastfield) approaches Kilmarnock box with an engineer's train heading to Hillhouse Quarry, near Barassie. The area to the right is now Hunslet Barclay Works, which recently merged to become Wabtec Rail Scotland. Note the John Walker factory also in the background, which was closed in 2013. Taken May 1984.

DMU Class 104, set 450, at Brownhill with the 15.35 Glasgow Central–Ayr service. The car in the background was my old Triumph Dolomite of 1979 vintage. The disused embankment behind the train was the flyover that brought the Kilbarchan Loop line back to join the main line. This was closed in 1972. Taken June 1984.

A three-car Class 104 DMU, now painted in standard BR blue/grey livery, at Ayr with the 19.28 service to Stranraer Harbour. These units provided a sterling service around Ayrshire before being transferred to Glasgow Eastfield depot in 1987. Taken August 1984.

EMU No. 314216 (Glasgow Shields) at Kilwinning on a test run. Class 314s do not normally work in Ayrshire. The unit had been on a test run to check the brakes and had run from its home depot of Shields; it is seen here preparing to return home. Taken May 2010.

No. 40122/D200 (Carlisle Kingmoor) at Pennyburn, south of Kilwinning, with the Macclesfield Largsman railtour heading to Largs. No. 40122 was later saved from the scrap man and went on to be part of the National Rail Museum collection at York. Taken August 1984.

A two-car Class 108 DMU at Kirkconnel with a service from Carlisle. Trains were terminating and starting from Kirkconnel this day due to engineering operations in the Mauchline area. Taken December 1984.

Class 121 DMU No. ADB 97058 (Glasgow Eastfield) at Bogside, north of Irvine, on a driver training run. These single railcars worked out of various depots initially and could be found almost anywhere in central Scotland. By this time, though, most had been scrapped or sent back down south to English depots. The few that remained, such as this one, were allocated to Eastfield depot in Glasgow. Note the Scotty dog symbol on side of unit. Taken May 1985.

A three-car Class 120 DMU at Girvan, having arrived with the 15.06 service from Ayr. These units were drafted in from Derby and Cardiff due to ongoing problems with Class 107 axles. Most were withdrawn in September 1986 when electrics took over the main Glasgow–Ayr workings. Some, however, were transferred to Edinburgh Haymarket. Taken March 1986.

A six-car Class 120 DMU at Kilwinning with the 15.15 Glasgow Central–Largs service. To me, these Class 120 units were almost as good as the old Class 126 Inter-City sets. Unfortunately, only one trailer survived into the preservation era. Taken March 1986.

DMU No. 143021 (Heaton Newcastle) stabled at Ayr Townhead. The unit had been built at Hunslet Barclay in Kilmarnock and was awaiting onward movement to Newcastle for use on local services there. Taken February 1986.

EMU Class 318s at Ayr station. These were the early days, when the end gangways were still in use and the Strathclyde orange livery prevailed. The Strathclyde livery lasted until 1999/2000 and was replaced by Strathclyde cream and red. Class 318s now receive overhauls at Doncaster and are emerging in the new Scotrail saltire livery. Taken August 1987.

No. 86230 *The Duke Of Wellington* (Willesden, London) at Ayr with the Royal Scot, the 07.45 Ayr–London Euston via Glasgow Central service. This served as a useful commuter service to Glasgow as well as an Inter-City service. However, this service was axed in 1993 when Inter-City took over the service from BR. Taken August 1987.

No. 50036 (Old Oak Common, London) and No. 50009 (Laira, Plymouth) at Bowhouse, south of Kilmarnock, between Hurlford and Mauchline with the Hoover Dambuster railtour heading back to Birmingham New Street. The railtour had come to Glasgow via the West Coast Main Line and was returning south via the Glasgow and South Western Main Line. This was the first time Class 50s had been over the G&SW since 1976. Taken May 1988.

No. 90002 (Willesden, London) arrives at Kilwinning with the 06.00 Glasgow Central–Ayr service. On arrival at Ayr, this would become the Royal Scot departing Ayr at 07.45 for London via Glasgow Central. Taken August 1988.

Seven-car Class 108 DMU passes Ayr depot with a day-return excursion from Ayr to Windermere. Foreign DMUs were rare to Ayrshire on excursions, and this was one of the few to visit. Taken April 1989.

Nos 20212 and 37376 (Both Glasgow Eastfield) at Auchincruive, east of Ayr, with a Knockshinnoch–Ayr Harbour loaded coal working. This unusual combination was because of a Class 37 failure. Taken May 1989.

No. 37071 (Immingham) inside Ayr depot between duties. Sadly, DBS pulled the plug on the depot in 2010, and at the end of 2014 all track was removed. Taken May 1987.

No. 26038 (Glasgow, Eastfield) on the Hillhouse Quarry branch with ballast hoppers. This line branched off the Barassie–Kilmarnock line east of Barassie, and was used until 2001. Taken April 1989.

Classes 37 and 20 locos stabled at Ayr depot. The leading unit 37 looks as if it could do with a good clean. In the early 1990s as many as twelve to fifteen Class 37s could be found around the depot at weekends in between duties. Taken June 1989.

No. 20903 *Lorna* and No. 20902 *Nancy* stabled in Barclays Yard, Kilmarnock. These locos were refurbished by Barclays and then hired to BR to carry out weed killing duties for a number of years. Some of them still survive with DRS at Carlisle Kingmoor depot. Taken May 1990.

Pacer No. 141101 (Leeds, Nelville Hill) stabled at Hunslet, Kilmarnock. This unit had been brought up from Leeds for bogie and engine overhaul. Taken June 1989.

Nos 37675 and 37676 (Both Glasgow Eastfield) at Annbank Junction with a loaded coal train from Killoch to Ayr Harbour. The shunter has de-trained and is about to operate the ground frame to allow the train off the branch to join the main line back to Ayr Harbour. Taken May 1994.

Nos 37670 and 37673 (both Plymouth Laira) depart from Irvine Caledonian pulp mill with the thrice-weekly 'silver bullets', as they were known, which ran to Burngullow in Devon. At the time this was the longest freight working in the UK. Taken March 1990.

No. 26035 (Glasgow Eastfield) approaches Prestwick Town with the 14.00 Carlisle–Ayr service. There would be no train heat or lighting as this was a freight only loco. Taken June 1990.

No. 156514 (Glasgow Corkerhill) near Mauchline with the 11.10 Carlisle–Glasgow Central service. Taken September 2012 (fisheye shot).